By ERICA GARCIA

ILLUSTRATED BY ELIOT ALEXANDER

"God Gave me a Free Tan!" Garcia, Erica

Summary: Based on a true story. Love Lee has a difficult experience at school. She overcomes the unhappiness of her incident, with the help of her parents. Love Lee shows us that friends come in all colors.

ISBN 13: 978-0-615-33242-0

FOR JASMINE AND HEAVEN

THANK YOU FOR TEACHING ME WHAT
TRUE LOVE REALLY IS.

FOR MOM

THANK YOU FOR
ENCOURAGING ME.

ACKNOWLEDGMENTS:

BRENDA COCHRIN: EDITOR

"Bye Ma," said Love-Lee on her way out to school.

"Big day at school today kids! Today is our Super Fun Day party," said Mrs. Swan. "Yea!" The whole class yelled all together as if it had been rehearsed.

"You will all need to pick a partner for our next game," said Mrs. Swan.

"Would you be my partner?" asked Love. "I can't" said Molly. "I am not allowed to play with you because you are brown." "What colors are you allowed to play with?" asked Love, as Molly walked away.

Love did not know why she felt so sad. She didn't feel like being brown was bad. Love didn't feel like playing with the class anymore. So, she went back to her desk to find out what made Molly think brown was bad.

Love sat at her desk, took out her crayon box and scribbled with every color she had. But there was nothing wrong with her brown crayon. She began to think about all the cool things that are brown. After all, She loved chocolate and it was brown.

When Love came home from school that day, She went into the bathroom to see if she could wash her brown away.

"What are you doing?" asked Love's Mom as she passed by. "Molly can't play with me because I'm brown, so I'm going to wash my brown away." said Love.

Love's Mom then took her into her room. "Sit down here and close your eyes" she said.

Love's Mom began to paint her face purple. "Do you feel any different?" she asked.

"No, I still feel like me," answered Love.

Love Lee ran to show her Dad. She wanted to know if he would like her better brown or purple.

"Daddy, Look at me," said Love. "Do you like me best brown or purple?" she asked.

"You look beautiful any color," he answered.

"Come with me Love, I want to show you something."

Love's Dad took her for a car ride.

When they arrived inside, there were big machines and people lying inside them.

"Why are they napping inside the bed with lights?" asked Love.

"This is a tanning salon. People come here and they pay to be brown just like you." said Love's Dad.

"So you see Love,
God gave you a free tan!"

On the next day of school, Molly asked Love if they could be friends. Love and Molly became B.F.F.'s.

And they both lived
happily ever after.

~The End~

DEAR LOVE

ALWAYS REMEMBER THAT WHATS IN YOUR HEART IS FAR MORE IMPORTANT THAN WHAT TOU WEAR.

A note to parents and teachers:

Although a difficult and sometimes uncomfortable topic to   address, discrimination and prejudice can and do affect children's lives. This affect goes far beyond hurt feelings, but can damage character, lower self-esteem and can break the spirit of a child. Children are lead by example. By sharing stories like this we will send a powerful message of love, understanding and respect for one another. We will build character and empower children. I was once told that if you have found one friend in a lifetime, you have accomplished something and that a good friend near by, is better than a brother far off. Please let's teach our children to love one another no matter what color!

Thank you for reading!